# SOLO CONCERT

# Solo Concert

## poems

Diana Senechal

SERVING
HOUSE
BOOKS

Solo Concert, poems
Copyright © 2025 Diana Senechal
First Edition

All rights reserved. No part of this book may be reproduced or transmitted in any form or by any means, electronic, digital, or mechanical, including photocopy, audio recording, or any information storage and retrieval system, without prior permission from the publisher or author (except by reviewers who may quote brief passages).

Front cover art adapted from Wassily Kandinsky, *Levels* (1929), *Wikimedia Commons*.

Published by Serving House Books
Lawrence Landing Company
Raleigh, North Carolina 27609
United States of America

www.servinghousebooks.com

Serving House Books is proud member of

Independent Book Publishers Association

and

Community of Literary Magazines and Presses

Paperback ISBN: 978-1-947175-63-1

Library of Congress Control Number: 2024947548

# SERVING HOUSE BOOKS

# CONTENTS

Foreword

## Part I: Solo Concert

| | |
|---|---|
| Solo Concert | 1 |
| After the Play | 2 |
| Hiding Places | 3 |
| Cigarettes | 5 |
| A Concert at the Reformed Music Festival... | 7 |
| Almost Late | 8 |
| Day of Rage | 10 |
| The Kernel Taboo | 13 |
| Letters from a Doll | 14 |
| Adventure | 16 |
| Typing Backwards | 17 |
| Listening | 19 |

## Part II: Off and On

| | |
|---|---|
| Off and On | 23 |
| The God of More | 25 |
| Goodbye to a Guitar | 26 |
| Document | 27 |
| Echoes of Sparrows | 28 |
| The Bargain | 29 |
| Too Serious | 30 |
| Upside Down | 32 |
| Productivity | 34 |
| The Misunderstanding | 35 |
| Entertainment | 36 |
| Thunder | 37 |

## Part III: Afternoon Visit

| | |
|---|---|
| Afternoon Visit | 41 |
| The Secret Park | 43 |
| The Speech | 44 |
| Zoetropes | 45 |
| Tuesday Evening in Fort Tryon Park | 47 |
| Air Without Crossing | 48 |
| The Corridor King | 49 |
| What to Do in These Circumstances | 51 |
| Dedication | 52 |
| J Train in September | 53 |
| Misplaced Fall | 54 |
| Pilgrimage in Winter | 55 |

## Part IV: Coffee Psalm

| | |
|---|---|
| Coffee Psalm | 59 |
| Jackrabbit | 60 |
| The Swing | 62 |
| Weathered Banderole | 64 |
| Embarking from Libau | 66 |
| The Life and Death (and Life) of Galoom | 67 |
| Looking Glass | 69 |
| Notes for a Course in Phonology | 71 |
| Reunion | 73 |
| Ride Home | 74 |
| Tower Song | 75 |
| Upon Returning from a Leave of Absence | 76 |

Credits and Acknowledgements
About the Author

# FOREWORD

The poems in this collection all have to do, directly or indirectly, with music. Each of the four parts corresponds roughly with an era of my writing (with exceptions), from the most recent poems to my college years. I wrote the title poem, "Solo Concert," in Hungary in early 2024; the last poem, "Upon Returning from a Leave of Absence," came out of John Hollander's Advanced Verse Writing seminar, which I took in 1988 as an undergraduate at Yale College. A few of the poems have been previously published; the credits appear at the end.

The forms include sonnets, villanelles, sestinas, syllabic verse, and free verse. The influences, preoccupations, rhymes, and themes vary, but they all seem to be of a bundle.

For the rest, the poems will speak for themselves.

Diana Senechal
Szolnok, Hungary
September 9, 2024

# Part I: Solo Concert

## Solo Concert

Our silence wove its way into the chords.
Ending and ending again, their color
lingered and deepened; even out the door,
they curled around us, bare guitar-words.
I was happy that night—but what is happy?
Performing, you were not, or so you said:
tense and under the weather, you knotted
a work-ladder up the songs, the wired sky.
I heard a joy there somewhere. Not a temple
gilded in slapdash gold. Not even felt
in space and time. Like a suspended fourth,
a dimension. No reckoner of worth
tallies this secret pasture. Figures melt.
Even the knots untie. The night goes simple.

## After the Play

Lined up for paradise? Then strip your pity
and toss it in the bin beside the stage.
In pity we play hero. Then our words
tumble and flail upon themselves, *but how,*
you plead, *could I have known?* Let's make the past
a stagelight. Have you ever, sable-brushed,
soaked up another's tears and daubed the wall
with icons of yourself on Mount Compassion,
glyphs heralding your name? Or a lowland
version of this? I have too—we're all suckers
for slop-heroics—but the edge of heaven
translates into a terse agreement with
the rim of words, the steps of dark. When you
fumbled (out in the air, hundreds attending),
I saved neither your endings nor your mood
but sank into your naked rendering,
your jumbled forms. *If there's no room to fail,*
a sage said, *it's not theatre.* I took
that not as: failure brings success (what is
that, anyway?), not even: art is risk,
but rather: failure becomes holy when
it breaks us open poor. I stand up from
the lower stone and walk. My shadow sheds
its garments and, like others going home,
lengthens across the green. The night bows low.
Goodbye for now. You too are all that is.

# Hiding Places

Everyone who knows you knows
your downhill slope: your poetry reading
in the wind, pages flying, you not knowing
your own poems, so after a few vain dashes
after the leaves, you cut it short, sorrying
sheepishly like so many other times, yet
we told you it was great, because it really
was: those three minutes or so when you
seized a form and vice versa, the bright
brief grip of eyes, words, and wind.
We believe in those three minutes, even now
that they have pared themselves down
to two and a half—even there we glean
a sanctum in what must be the worst
torque of despair: watching yourself flee from
your own soul, not being able to chase yourself
down that elusive tube. "We," I say,
but the crowds have dwindled as well,
down to the few wild-haired ones you long
ago wrote off as old hat. So you leave
us behind and slink into cooler throngs,
who have no clue how this will all fly
apart and where no one expects you
to be gifted or even good. Smoky blue air,
comfort of nobodiness. I saw you there
one evening—finding solace there too—
and left you alone, didn't even tap my feet
in time with yours, waited until you had gone
and come from the bar before buying
my next beer, because, illusion or not,

it is the sense of something in common
that swells up in me like a psalm, so that I
too have leaves slipping from me, I too
chase them on a lark, then call it off,
stop still, and let the praise hail down
on me, pelting my pate. It's a good feeling,
and if it wounds, I slink away to my den.
Praised, you sang, praised be the hiding places.

## Cigarettes

People frowned on them; that was their delight.
Those who didn't belonged to a tight club
who sinned together, glowing in silence
or flicking an ash or two, a sparse bond
in the cold. Some of my best friends were made
out there. Hard to explain. Don't friends desire
the best for you, like health? Yes, but even
more did we want truth. Not that our embers
kindled honest words, but the shared smoke breaks
gave us a way of gathering without
putting up fronts. True, this too was a kind
of smokescreen, but we didn't know it yet.

Mainly we hated being nagged, I think.
Smoking felt like a big "fuck you," a phrase
I relished at the time. The more you told
me I should quit, the more I smoked. Now I
see the folly in this, but even so
I rail against the brittle shield of "should"—
which, to exist, objects to who I am
and what I do—but, you might ask, don't I
have "shoulds" of my own, things I want to be
but fall short of? Or wish upon the world?
Yes, but such "shoulds" require a counterpoint.
I'll tell you a short tale to make my point.

In an old town, a young man lived alone
and taught robotics at the public school.
At night he played guitar. He had no phone,
no friends. His neighbors called him "April fool."
The reason: caked boots (spring was muddy there).

He'd knock and scrape them, leave them by the door,
but locals mocked him for his single pair;
anyone but a hobo would buy more.
One day he moved away. You know the rest,
or part of it: he found both love and fame.
Nothing had changed about the way he dressed;
by all counts he had stayed mostly the same.

A moral beckons, but I let it be.
Wisps of wisdom no longer dazzle me.

# A Concert at the Reformed Music Festival on Bakáts Square, Budapest

What carried me from zero to one?
Wings marrowed with the knowledge
(inexplicable) that I had to come.
You know it: when your feet lift
you out the door, fatigue and cough
be damned, and the train clatters
to a beat it never tested until now.

The rain tiptoed, then gave in, tumbling
to songs of spiral, forest and plunge.
Infinity swinging from leafy chords.
The night before, a crowd of thousands
thrummed to the cadence of these songs.
Today we were fewer, but why make idols
of numbers crumbling as we speak?

We had all been standing or sitting
some polite meters away from the stage,
sopping, absorbed, when someone declared,
"heck, to heaven with it!" and clambered close.
We all followed suit, huddling together
under several umbrellas. "Gyere, gyere
közelebb," a woman insisted, holding hers

over me. I gave in, all the rebels did,
lightning, grief, the sun dark as a zero,
to where no one could claim the sky
didn't know these songs by heart, hadn't
borne them for aeons, or that any of us
had contours that could confidently boast,
*I am impervious to God's watercolor.*

## Almost Late

My school isn't far
from home; biking, I fuss less
than I would by car.

Sometimes a cirrus
cloud glides over me, a puff
of teased animus.

Once I shot a rough
draft of its tail with my phone.
It wasn't enough;

for that wispy gnome
risking lateness, I stood taut
till I spied a lone

crow lift and besot
the hour with its dark vowel.
Speed-biking, I caught

up with the school bell
barely, making the long way
shortest after all.

If I get away
with this once more, I will speak
its virtues one day:

Praised be the bright break.
Praised the empty interlude
by the tongue-tied lake—

but that might seem rude
to those who seek dignity
in disquietude,

who labor with glee,
mumbling digits to their god,
productivity.

Still I give a nod
to that sanctum, for without
sin, my thrill would rot

into a rank doubt:
an annoying lack of car
and a roundabout.

## Day of Rage

From the first morning tremor of my toes,
I recognized this as the day of rage,
so I arose at dawn to choose the cloth
to wear up to the highest nearby hill
with hopes of being heard by the bored sky.

A red dress? No, that would knock the wind
out of my words, and I meant to be heard.
The deep blue one was of the essence now,
the one the sky had dropped on me by chance.
That was to be the vestment of my rage.

As for shoes, sneakers would have to do.
Who cares how the feet look when their role
is just to take me up the mount of rage?
There it's the mouth that matters; pure ire
has no release except through syllable,

so I brushed my teeth and guzzled half a liter
of sparkling water to levitate my thoughts.
Time to set out. The hill I chose was some
twenty kilometers away. I took the bike,
even at risk of burning off some spleen,

and pedaled up it, proud to have arrived
at the place in life where I can finally say
exactly what I mean, unsanded by
shame or apology, just the words
that fall loose from the craters of the mind.

But what came out wasn't at all like rage.
First, nothing. I looked around the droopy
still-waking fields and thought it might be rude
to rush their rhythms all for the sake of my
sloppy paean to problems shared by none.

Then, when I kicked away that sham excuse
(what do the fields care?) and began to sing,
I saw that there were other hills nearby,
each of them topped with someone a bit like me,
staking their day on a hope of being heard,

and then I knew. Even now, even
with every ounce of ire my will could cast
into a form of sound, whatever, whoever
it was that hadn't answered me before
wouldn't be shaken into answering.

Worse still, I wasn't mad. Nor were the others
who cried on dots of hills from sea to sea.
This is where music comes from, the unanswered
prayer, text message, private turn of thought,
this cry into the vault that turns away.

Had our hills been closer, our eyes might possibly
have met. We might have spent the day together:
skies to each other, forests interleaving,
words interchanging, tempered in their timing,
finding their harmony in joined rage.

"But you just said there was no rage!" No,
I said I wasn't mad. That's not the same.
The rage is everywhere. I'm going home,
but tomorrow I'll get up early again,
put on a different dress, head for the hill,

and thrill up there with all the holy gadflies,
and maybe, one blind day, the rage will sing
such thunder that the sky will clap and smile,
and I will do the same, grinning the news
that I, too, am the vault that turns away.

# The Kernel Taboo

The word "you" has become suspicious.
If I pronounce it, is it *you* I mean?
Does it point to the existence of us?

When I let it loose, you roared, "Cut the fuss!"
(a different "you," a stranger dressed in green).
The word "you" struck "you" as suspicious.

I try to walk my words past the rumpus
erupting where a naked soul is seen.
(Does it hint at the existence of us?)

Babbling, I stumble. My rude habitus
misses the stars. A crash, a smithereen.
The word "you" loiters nearby, suspicious,

but no one arrests it; supercilious,
it leans against the wall of what has been.
I think it might know something about us.

Look back at me, let us not be gracious
to the grave! Why shut up what you have seen?
Say "you" to me, speak the suspicious,
and nothing will be left to dread but us.

## Letters from a Doll

A girl had lost her doll; to help her through,
Kafka wrote letters—from the doll—that told
where she had been, what she had learned, and what
learning, if not what lessons, lie in loss.
Later the girl found one more in a crack:
*Love will come back, but in a different form.*

Loss let us first define as ruptured form.
Everything hails from it; it bellows through
the vaults of dark and stars, shaking a crack
in light itself, untelling what was told
and starting a new story: *I am loss;
in me there is no who, where, why, or what.*

I didn't know my winding words were what
wore out your own, or that I broke a form;
I thought I'd never be a source of loss.
But loss lies in all things, soaking them through,
down to the dearest, down to what we told
ourselves was firm, down to the plastered crack.

Late in the attic, looking through the crack
in the pine wall, I think I make out what
could be your afterlight. A singer told
me once that certain songs attain their form
from being listened to, and even through
full stoppage can be heard. So with your loss,

so with the fading of the light, the loss
of stuff and all its traps, the faithful crack
in hoped-for shapes, the senses dimming through
lowest degrees, down into who knows what,
the hints of weather marks and final form,
hushing to null, in what the pinewood told.

Yes, the beloved story comes untold
through being heard; nothing without its loss,
it casts me out of what I thought was form.
I rotate this black box, trying to crack
its terse domain, to learn, if lucky, what
keeps it from falling open, being through.

Instead, I hear a form of letter. Told
through a new face, cast in new sound, the loss
becomes a pause, a crack, a question, *what?*

## Adventure

It has become pollyannish to say,
"Every morning I wake up into a
new adventure"—we feel a duty to
groan perfunctorily, curse the day just
enough to avoid the eyerolls and barbs
of our co-workers and acquaintances.
We therefore take care to don an airtight
layer of rayonish pejoratives.

Still I refuse to be hemmed in by
what others think—an adventure's nothing
to sneer at—and, by the way, do you have
any clue what I have beheld on mine?
Beheld: a word worth saying more than once.
I have beheld thousands of leaves, each with
its own trace, its own mix of veins, colors,
and crinkles. Our tragic diversity.

"Tragic" is no defect, though: a fixture
of the play is that it starts promptly at eight,
I must occur, yet my missteps will beat
an ancient warning or a song's compass.
Come, will you join me, dare the great mistake?
There's laughter in it too; there's everything.
You do not need a rainbow to see this
shimmer of time, this nothing, these waters.

# **Typing Backwards**

Now is the time to talk. I don't mean
dipping my bread into your clipped glyphs
and gobbling like a tramp, or stirring shock
and awe into our first long-distance tea.
I mean the simple conference. The back
and forth that all the world has come to miss.

What I have never known, how can I miss?
Without matter, how can I find a mean?
I too have walked my mind and fingers back
to our first meeting, where your hymnous glyphs
shook me from lullaby. Instead of tea,
I drank the beauty of the limpid shock.

Later, I only partly meant to shock
you and others; most of that swing-and-miss
came from my gait. A sitting down for tea
would have made you and me a bit less mean.
Instead I racked my mind over my glyphs,
wishing I could reshape them, roll them back

across the border. Yet the taking back
would fade into the page. My fingers shock
the keys, and they shock back; the stoic glyphs
have long known these erasures. "You will miss
our mark," they say. But cuts mark too (I mean
the million times I backspaced on a T).

You think I'm playing with infinity?
Last year, maybe. Not now. No going back
to that old cant. Sometimes I was a mean
mortality protester. I would shock
the rosy wellness-hawkers with my mis-
creant letters, my ever-stretching glyphs.

Now it's all one. The river thrums my glyphs
into the easeless day. A spill of tea
lifts ink from the old diaries. I miss
missing itself, the feeling, far far back
in the blue past, that words of truth and shock
would become flesh. At least conjure your mien.

Now I see what I missed: your cryptic glyph
speaks its own mean. "To keep your dignity,
hold something back." So I delete the shock.

# Listening

Today I tried something new
(Or old in a new way):
Saying nothing.

True, many stints of null
Had marked my days before,
But this nothing had

A pluck to it.
Tuning, muting
Its strings, gearing

Up for the miracle
(As anything that comes
From zero is miracle),

It befriended the oval.
Later I thought of how
The hush had given me time

To hear space sing,
To see the clouds converge,
Break up, glitter, and

Spatter the long sands,
Daring me into a brief
Collapse of words.

The words resurged,
But with the glint of return
From a private voyage:

"Later I looked up the name
Of that beach whose waves
Rough-sang the sky."

# Part II: Off and On

# Off and On

I shuffled out of my slippers
and curled my toes into the pine.

Someone else, having donned
them, now heads out onto

the early hour-lit stones
in the steam of rain, the blur

of a day hesitating with form.
I do not long after them.

What are those slippers? you ask.
What do they represent?

Ah, something you'll never
guess—that's the whole point—

because I'm still wearing them,
still need them, still find warmth

in their matted plush, wouldn't
lose them for the world

(well, maybe for some piece
of the world, but not all of it;

no one in their corrected
mind wants everything).

There is something in each
of us that moves and stops,

both at once, that loses
forever and forever keeps.

Soft be the soles that tap
the perpetual barefoot beat.

## The God of More

I once worshiped the god of more,
the robot drum chopping the night,
not programmed to stop for breath,
the wave roaring over your name
with ebbless, pelagic will,
the hand taking hold of a shoulder,
numb to the pulling away,
the cry that spills on your shoes,
then calls for another beer.

There is a pause
that lets music rustle itself
gently into its clothes.

There is a love
that lives by not having to have.

But no, this is not a sermon.
Things come to an end anyway.
Come, look at the dwindling gold.

## Goodbye to a Guitar

Goodbye and getting rid are not the same.
I lift you up and lay you in your case;
you echo as though hollowed of my claim.

I played you rarely and I played you tame,
but still you rumbled forth your chordal lace.
Goodbye and getting rid are not the same.

I strum amiss and try to slap the blame
by rapping on the crack that splits your face.
You echo as though hollowed of my claim.

One day, in chords alone, you asked my name,
which might have spelled an end to this embrace.
Goodbye and getting rid are not the same.

"I could have dropped you in a dump of shame,
brushed off my pants, and shrugged at your disgrace,"
you echo, as though hollowed of my claim.

O may you play in sweet strong hands, in fame
or home, and may my ear pick up a trace—
goodbye and getting rid are not the same—
.....
You echo, as though hollowed of, my claim.

# Document

Fame isn't fun, I've learned from brief blasts of it,
and yet we're told it's fun, told that those who
grab it deserve to be bowed down to or at least
envied with all the green our skin can muster.
When I got famous one hour, I couldn't answer
the kindest messages properly. I would start
to write something, then stop. The fame, though,
danced on my tongue; later, when it already
had lost its fizz, I dropped a seltzer tablet into it,
stirred it up, said, behold, if you didn't catch
it earlier, you still can. But it tasted metallic.
I dumped it and took a walk. Evening had snuck
in without asking. I watched a mess of twigs
crisscross the clouds parading past the moon
and glimpsed the latter peeking and hiding again
like a baby new to the game. The moon didn't
giggle, though, which meant something had
gone solemn, something had to swell into a risk
or shrivel forever. You don't have to do it,
I told myself, but that rang feeble: the thing
had already clenched its fist in me, clotted
into old blood. Gentler tasks awaited me too,
lots of them, but first: sit down, sign the deed.
*I hand over my lifelong semblances.*

## Echoes of Sparrows

Stop, gossips: before your knee-tongues jerk
out into "snob," consider who you name,
think of her easy gliding up the same
stairway you throng down onto. Try to work

some silence for a change; notice her own,
the way she harbors thought, her gently cold
turn of the head, her shroud. Your overtold
rumors make petty clatter; glancing down

barely, she laughs, not like a brittle queen
weary of her rude realm, but like a boy
who sees his checkmate move. Those who enjoy
solving puzzles may know of her demesne,

which worships only the divinity
of doing well, where art, clothes, syllables
blaze calm through meme and slogan. Dogma falls,
will always fall, against infinity.

I too have wondered how such equipoise
can fill a woman, so that all your names,
rumors, and taunts—even your gilded fames
and praises—fizzle into wisps of noise.

Maybe a brutal grief taught her the cost
of stooping even slightly for the sake
of pleasing. Maybe she turned mistake
into magnificence. But having lost

a thing or two, I want for once to live
up to the dark and say: I do not know.
You say you'll pay me if I say I know,
but I say no. I want for once to live.

## The Bargain

After the play, the hall's souls
keep custom: hand against hand
in upscale synchronization,
bows (the "ow" kind), more bows,
an empty stage, an aw-shucks return,
the aged bard now among them,
whistles, perfunctory thunder,
then the well-timed fizzle, meaning
the hour holds sway now, it's ten.
Even she dares not seize the
bullion, leap to her feet, cry
"wonderful, wonderful!"—after all,
what does "wonderful" mean, why
foist a debt on strangers: either
they remain seated (insulting
the players) or lose more of
their night. She heeds the mean,
claps within brackets, shudders
as a chalice topples, smashing
the dark: a clatter, then later
the scattered motto of shards:
here we die again, having paid
to behold and not to become.

## Too Serious

They took their baby to the oracle
down by the river bank, under the bridge,
who said, "Your daughter is too serious,
well, not too serious, but serious,
which in the world's eyes is too serious."
They tore their hair and sank their frantic souls
and savings into schools and counselors.
She learned the daintihoods of lady-lite:
to curl her certainties with "I don't know,"
to bounce her questions on a lilt of tongue,
to add a smiley to each thank-you note.
They laughed to see their fear fizzle away.

One day she fell into a brouhaha
at the train station, with a stranger—well,
what of it? No one heard or saw the scene
except her tutor, who penned down her shouts
in some blue diary, filled otherwise
with canny formulas and apothegms.
She shook it off as she had learned to do,
travelled to her exam, which she had meant
to pass just barely, but excelled upon,
a thing to laugh about, to dine over,
to raise a raucous glass to, as the glint
fizzles into the deep encaving fear.

Years later, months of quest carried her to
the oracle, who took her in his arms,
invited her to stay the afternoon,
and then fell mum. There on the table lay
a pencil and a sharpener. She took
and worked them in her hands, amazed by the
ringlets of falling wood. Sideways she saw
his own eyes fixed upon the gleaming point
that grew more distant as the curls of dross
kept falling, falling. Started from his daze,
he swallowed twice, as if about to speak,
but she had risen to her ken and gone.

## Upside Down

To have been invited
to the party at all
surprised and dazzled him,

so he put on a tie,
then changed his mind, opted
for his London-grey tee,

set out the door, slowed his
pace so as not to seem
too eager, walked around

the block twice, took a breath,
rang the bell, waited, and
pushed when he heard the buzz.

He thought no one would brave
his face of moss and bricks
but a few sized him up

with the skeptical "Do
you actually *know*
them? *Personally?*" Not

wanting to brag, he shrugged:
we're acquaintances, we've
talked now and again. *"Ah,*

that explains *everything*.
Well it sure is a fun
party, isn't it? What

was your name again?" He
almost told them but knew
it would slip through their ears

(the party held only
a few bigwigs; the rest
were just droplets who would

seep through the boards into
the downstairs subletters'
living room, join the chunks

of plaster, hit the rare
silk rug—a shriek, then the
whirr of humdrum cleanup).

So instead he looked this
way and that for the hosts
but saw them in bright-eyed

rapturous talk that seemed
much too heart-to-heart to
break into. He shuttered

his eyes and gathered up
something inside him like
a hand-me-down of song,

then started back downstairs,
home on his mind. Even
the upside-down party

would have marveled at the
sure cadence of his steps,
the sober, resplendent

sense of time being up:
of having to rise up
now, for good, if ever.

## Productivity

When I bemoan the little I have done
from dawn to dusk—the promises unkept,
story unfinished, kitchen floor unswept
panning my conscience like a pantheon;
when, looking for some task to seize upon
and nail, only to find each one adept
at leaping from my hands (the laundry crept
away, I chased it, and it split and won),
I only have to listen to one song—
go ahead, call me lazy, call me lame—
to know the day repaid a thousand loans,
because all songs need listeners; their fame
occurs in quiet, and whatever wrong
occasioned them, a twain of ears atones.

## The Misunderstanding

The room rang loud, so after spurts of *what*s
and *I-can't-hear-you*s, I declaimed a tale,
doused with illusion, of a bowl of kale
all crinkly somber green, sprinkled with nuts
and lush tomatoes.... where from here? A klutz
with small talk, stumped beyond the pale,
I nailed the salad part, but when the frail
rundown ran out, I flailed in *and*s and *but*s.

And while you smiled, and while the evening's breath
released into a breeze, and I believed
that every nod of audience you meant,
that, just as I poured forth with the intent
of giving, so with gift was I received,
I was deceived, and you were bored to death.

## Entertainment

More light, but not from you! the neighbors warn.
They praise the bargain bulbs that stud the fence
but shield their faces from your starry eyes.
Too bright, they say, too nervy, out of size—
dim them a bit (the eyes), and they might earn
a chance to serve as party ornaments.
By blazing on, you show your meager care
for their injunctions or the bitter air.
How do you stand full fire where fire is banned?
Why would they want a middling neighborhood?
Why do they hover by the buzzing light?
Asking myself these things, I stood the night,
each hour an age, until I understood;
that is, I age and still don't understand.

## Thunder

Crash of word, afterlight,
shatterer of afternoons,
when you come again,

rouse the rain, hurl it all
the way down to our embalmed
corpse of compromise.

Ken your way there and back,
cross the firmament and bell-
ow your jagged streak,

not to be calligraphed,
nor fit for parenthesis;
end the otherwise.

Good the life that dares re-
sound: I awoke to and lost
two shivers of bright

reckoning; nonetheless,
this last chance blazes mythic
through all that went wrong.

# Part III: Afternoon Visit

# Afternoon Visit

*In memory of John Hollander*

The slow and steady lever of the sun
turned branches into peacocks by the window.
The fires across the sky pulled blue and yellow
from grass and pines; a tilting cypress bole
pulled purple in reply. We spoke of Hebrew,
of words that open into other words.

"Odeh la-El levav hoker" – those words
sang into other songs, and the long sun
lingered in lowering. What little Hebrew
I toted here dissolved into a window.
Your giant thought rose up, a stubborn bole
engraced by leaves that lifted into yellow.

I wait for you to wake; I watch the yellow
candle that chants for me in place of words.
The evening rolls itself into a bole
whose branches reach the final strokes of sun.
Just as I turn my wishes from the window,
an answer murmurs past my mind in Hebrew.

It puzzles me as I look up the Hebrew;
"zahav" – "gold," or maybe "tzahov" – "yellow."
Speak, arbiter! No help; the stolid window
declines to meddle in these jousts of words.
Jealous or luminous? The candle-sun
bows out of it; I think toward the bole.

I make my way outdoors, run to the bole,
and throw my arms around it: "Teach me Hebrew."
I wake back into faces past the sun:
crying or stoic, sleepless-dark or yellow,
they measure out and hide away their words,
then turn toward the doctor in the window.

He makes a cryptic gesture through the window
like branches with a message from the bole.
If you could speak, you'd riddle out the words,
and then we'd wend our way back into Hebrew,
and roots, and tropes, and Browning—all that yellow
and sound that fills the letters of the sun.

Sun overtakes the glare. The morning window
boasts yellow heaven, but the wizened bole
cracks, Hebrew, human, holy, into words.

# The Secret Park

Long-lost friend, where have you been?
Down to the valley to find my gown.
What valley? Brooklyn has no hills!
It does, when it lifts and lets down souls.
What kind of gown? Please fill me in!
The kind you marry, not marry in.
Marry a dress? The frills your groom?
No frills, just cloth from a chanting loom.
A prayer? Close. A rhythmic walk
with verse all the way to a broken park.
Crumbling leaves pardon the bench;
beetles plunder the rotten branch.
I said a rhyme and let it swing
as the breeze incanted each dying thing.
I gasped at the goodness not my own,
and the sun, too soon, ran under a stone.

## The Speech

From far away I heard you speak today,
the way we hear bells in a slant of sun,
knowing they ring at five—the calendar
itself makes words, the very rays make chords.

A teacher must have rushed there after school,
arrived breathless, flopped in a seat, arranged
her coat and hair, leaned into heed, and found
a rampart in the very listening.

Something to sit up for, something to hold
one's head up for, a time to put aside
one's foibles for, even a distant time,
this came my way today, a reckoning.
I grasped that there was loneliness in gold
and gold in air, and debt in everything.

## Zoetropes

Anything can be anything.
The midway point can be anything.
Identical ends meet.

I sleep on a stream of frames.
Stick figures, cars, spiders
shouting the colors ride.

Rivulet running in circles,
water falls down from my brain,
grandmother holding a baby.

Paper is not like music.
It's thick and material.
Mine I use as a hammock.

People are starting to die.
My friends are having children.
I'm still learning to talk.

Leaving a space open
for you to sit by me,
I join you in body code,

looking away, then back,
then into the nearby wall
where we were both once pictures.

Amazing how we have grown.
We can be anything:
acrobats, puppets, pets.

Words splash into our glasses.
The players have opened their cases.
The lights blast rude again.

All that can be has been.
In our split-second hug
my whirling comes to an end.

# Tuesday Evening in Fort Tryon Park

Evening bends into the leaves.
Breathing falls in with the river;
tablets break over and over.

Rock strains its nerves to endure,
flame lingers over the river,
prophets point over the border.

Song tumbles onto the path—
day is not, day is not over—
gardens stand tall against slumber.

Man, who are you to pass by,
flourishing into the ether,
vapor and structure together?

Teach me that this is not vain,
hasten the rising of favor.
Cedar and heather, start over.

Mystery, hint at your name.
Love, shed a drop of your silver;
chariot, rush me to shelter.

## Air Without Crossing

Air without crossing.
I'm tired of your tattoo
and the long, long taboo;

your crackling derision,
a ciggy and a sneer
on the sun-wiggly pier.

These words made of lesions—
if I venture past hello,
I'm in for a blow.

You scoff at communion.
You want a pretty neck
that wilts into heck.

So starve well and listen:
the no-no words will freeze
 themselves into keys.

Without even knowing,
you gave me real estate.
Free gab can be great,

but this is still greater:
a music room, a door,
some sounds and a floor.

This built-in forgiveness:
"Who enters here, be still."
Why, thank you. I will.

# The Corridor King

I stopped you in the hall for advice,
taller, but looking up to you,
older, but baby to your words.
Answers tumbled into my ears.

Giant, you swept away my thoughts.
With bull-deep voice and rustic legs
you told me the tale of taking time
to sort things out alone, etc.

I thanked you, beaming, tossing it all.
Perhaps I had caught a tone or two,
but even that had not been my plan.
I took in your counsel just to stand still

(a hard enough task when you're in the lead,
spooning out words to numbered minds).
I made you my mentor so I could rest
and slip out of my decision-dress.

The question concerned a cracking life,
where neither of us had special wit.
You knew the girl much better than I,
but I knew more from other sides.

I knew not only that I was the girl
(ha ha, did you guess it, later that night?)
but that it was you who had sought me out,
longing to play the corridor king.

And golden you loomed in my tiptoe farewell.
And foxy I bounced in your double-take,
a faceted tower—a frivolous dot—
we shook back into our clumsy frames.

Oh to be at ease for a little while,
whatever it takes. I lie, by the way.
We were a little more nervous than that,
taking turns speaking, shifting our legs.

## What to Do in These Circumstances

Dark water loads the clouds. Shall we slide down
the silver ropes, clink teacups in the crash,
run for our wits? Your face in splinter-flash
looks goddamn gorgeous—then a streak of frown
shatters the flimsy glass of tinker-town.
I tumble silent but I tumble rash,
gnashing my thoughts, for lack of else to gnash,
rolling around without a rule or gown.

When measure loses measure, that's called pride,
and that explains the slide.
It makes no sense but happens anyway.
I could load up the air with wails of why,
but that's as foolish as to say I'll try
to silently roll up my unsaid say.

## Dedication

I own no portion of the rain,
not the patter of gods on tin,
not the sheen of the swooshed coast,
not the pinnacle lost in mist.
I own not even the grey-stained
drizzle of dream on windowpane,
not the prayer on felled knees,
not the hush of the held soul.

Once, in a 4 a.m. refrain,
gift took over the tapping rain,
brooms swept over the bare boards,
making spirits of dropped words.
Ribbon circled the spare still
lone seconds. Fragile clock,
wrapped in tapping. Morning fell;
I clipped my way out into the world.

If I may give what is not mine,
pull the ribbon and take not mine.
If giving it should be a crime,
know I hovered around the crime.
I'd give, if I could give you time,
*that* time, *that* untrammeled time.
I'd even go to jail for time,
but taking, too, would be a crime.

# J Train in September

Sounds the first gong of fall.
I get in line
behind the cloud I know by shape as mine.
Like a shawl
it ripples with my shivers. Like a wolf
relieved of frame, unrolling from its growl,
it settles into a grey hush of self.

Clank, staircase to the train.
Who walks this way
must have been born to the same shape as I.
Pounding rain,
brother push, stranger veer. Hope swell and sag.
Now the old wisdom drops from the family line,
and I am left with my own bag to lug.

Doors close, chug starts.
They sit in groups,
crowing about the jerks who tore their coops.
Chicken arts,
rage of lost prison, yearning for the mesh,
pecking the earth in vain for petty cash,
not I, I lie. I come from different parts.

We get off at the same stop.
Our clumsy loads
bump here and there until they take their roads.
My grey-green hope
is for a tie of tongue, a pull of lake,
a taut, well-knotted story, and a break
from the loud loop, the grip of the group-rope.

## Misplaced Fall

It is not mine, this day
of six-month-misplaced fall,
yet I cram it with my stuff
and lug it back to the harbor where
the hopeful hum with flimsy trade
and never know to call enough enough
or a spade a spade.
Wares flare in thunderlight;
crooks crawl outside to play.
They dare us all to stake our share
on a phony sun, a dashed-off prayer
to a crummy god. Their bright
rocket blasts off, then plummets in the shade.
Such ships with their high haul
make streaks in minds as virtue pines
and dealers cast away.

I came out in this hush,
this humble rustle of your brother's end.
I have no salve, no song,
no stained and storied quilt.
All I have is a bag of varied cares.
I set it down and listen to the shore,
the roar of things I do not understand,
the hand, the rush, the tilt
where things went wrong.

## Pilgrimage in Winter

Praise for the hill and the cold air over the hill,
the stones on the hill, the stones on stones, the stone
in my hand. The one who moved me over the land,
may you rest well, brave soul; may blessings fall
on those you led from the cruelest fields and those
you helped bring forth. Great worker, receive this stone,
these feet, these tears. I will be leaving soon,
lest figures form or I start taking stock.
I know what Buber meant: measure has fled;
shadow and light have joined. There is no picture.
For a moment (where are its edges?) I was with you,
a moment past the fence around myself.

A fenceless hill it seemed, without a tree;
a glittering snow came down later that day
and blessed the stones. By then I had gone home,
but nothing was the same. I mean this not
in a colloquial sense. I mean: the desk
had lost its former purpose. Sitting to write,
I buoyed with words. I took a walk and sang
the snowfall, marveled at the marks of paws,
and thought again of clambering up that hill,
and praised the source of chill around my head.

It happens to you, and you walk alone.
This truth comes over you: this secret that
can never be a secret, as it's all
that has been known and all that can be known.
No, that's not true. My speck was just a speck;
against it, an encyclopedia
could still do well, I figure. All the same,
I walk bareminded to the end of love.

Thank you for the company of good prophets.
Thank you for the closed fountain underground.
Here is the weight of all that I have met;
here is the mark of dignity in stone.
Where, though, where are you? Memory wraps up,
unwraps again, and wraps, but finds hard air.

Stones there were many. The one I left behind
joined a sweet multitude but stayed alone.
Music is made of solitudes like this.
Somewhere, in the kindred air, there were songs.

A miracle, your life; a miracle
to meet a speck of it through hill and stone.

# Part IV: Coffee Psalm

## Coffee Psalm

Call it a dream: this morning, spilling over
the rim of baked containers, spiting fear,
rinsing away the pain of last night's beer,
spotting the stench-stained cloth, painting it over,
call it a dream, I'll dream it ten times over,
I'll hold it close, I'll let it disappear
into the bleak of day, since you, my dear
friendship, burst forth when signs declare you over:
not like auto-reverse, or auto-drip
(that sudden sputter of a hushed machine);
there's nothing automatic about magic.
It's not like anything; approaching rhymeless,
it bathes my head with tears that leave me clean,
and fills my mug as I, forgiven, sip.

# Jackrabbit

This land has never been painted properly.
Mix clumps of juniper with moonbeam blue,
Throw in a bit of tooth, a bit of song,
to fill the silhouette with bite and tongue.

This is a real dirt road with imagined rocks,
senses, insensate dangers, destinations.
Headlights sweeping the long floor of the mind
pan a jackrabbit back and forth in time.

Caught in the blank emergency of beams,
he dodges his dilemma with a brisk
"what if, what if" that dances him to death.
He could not find a way out of the way.

Earlier that day I was on the phone,
missing all your relevant advice.
A wire had got caught up in my throat,
an answer-dodger. It distracted me.

It trembled so fast that it numbed my tongue.
It did this while you were trying to talk.
I couldn't listen well because the dance
had blurred all trace of consonant and sense.

I think now that this may have been a crash
of my old givens against your offerings:
new junipers, or ways of seeing them,
new countries, or ways of getting there.

When I hung up, there was no wire or word.
The moon was gone, the road a long fur coat
on some unwitting wearer, blissed and hushed.
I forgot all about it until years later.

You had said: "You can go left or right."
Take me straight! I shouted. Straight to the remedy.
Gallop like the nineteenth century
down to the police station or cemetery.

Striding answerless, a station incarnate,
a cop ticketed me for not listening.
Now I can bear the rabbits and the wires.
I inch through forks and roadkill, listening.

## The Swing

There stood a swing by the edge of town
that lifted us over our lives.
It graced the ragged grass of a farm,
and the hired hand would pause and watch
as we kicked off into the blue,
one at a time, over the years,
swinging with nothing else in our eyes
but the edge of town and the sky.

This man had seen people come and go
and whole populations go.
Such memories rob your mind, he said;
they steal on you at any old hour
unless you have toils and cares.
So he tended the hens and watched the swing.
It was the swing, he said, that creaked
his ragged mind to repose.

I came here when in doubt of the world
or in search of a lift of view.
Dozens of others have done the same:
we swang and thought, swang and thought
our way into gilded mind.
All of us yearned for an edge of town,
a place to sit in the wind and song,
a place that, swaying, still stood.

Inside, the owners looked on the scene
that frothed and seethed in their eyes.
It's good, they mouthed, with our children grown,
that the swing has carried on for so long,
but look at the filth and the noise.
Tomorrow we'll take it down, they vowed.
And so it happened: overnight
a canticle dropped into time.

Not long ago I saw a swing
much like the one I had known.
It stood on a farm, removed from the road,
so I watched from afar, and it eyed me too,
as though we were both on display.
I shook my head and headed on.
Speech would have cost too much to repair,
and the hush was acceptably true.

## Weathered Banderole

I creaked into the hut; the splintered light
fell three ways, by my count: onto the spat,
the brewing, and the sparkling after-dust.
The particles danced with time, and I with them,
whirling across the planks, mindful of beams.

All particles will stop rotating someday,
but for the while we've got a few more spins
and yards of reel. I came a bit unsure,
but  how good, how unfettered to be here.
Then I unrolled your weathered banderole.

*You took my time*, you railed, at the time--
but after the invective scrawl ran dry,
time-robbers plagued you day by day until
you hurled into the planks, cursed at the beams,
and grasped at last that there had been no theft,

or else, more likely, it had been all theft,
each moment pilfered by a different hand,
and everyone to blame. Maybe your arm
couldn't sustain the finger any more;
maybe the will grew wobbly like the planks.

But blame me one more time, so I can say
*I'm sorry*, meaning all ten years of it,
and you can gulp and answer, *It's OK*.
Then I will creak my way back out the door
and leave you to your shortened afternoon

where orange rays make fire of every nail,
and velvet cushions loll around the room,
and by the bulb, a housefly shot with blue
beats tremors deep into the tape machine,
and all the hut reverses into dark.

# Embarking from Libau

The festive billows roll.
Random the rotten ships set sail,
young drunkards lean against the rail,
unschooled, unshaven, fresh from jail
and innocent of trial.
I'll stay with them awhile,
for I'm the man who nails the nail,
and mends the hull, and braves the gale.
I'll mend their fates from head to tail,
though I can't mend the soul.
Libau wises us well,
as Russia smirks beneath her veil
and promises to feed us ale
when we return from hell.
The laughing chapel bell
drowns out the wives, whose widowed wail
makes even stalwart captains flail
and tears apart the lull.
We'll drown the Japanese! All hail!
We'll mount each bloody skull
upon the mast of guile!
But marriage comes to null,
and Russia blushes under veil
as we set forth without a trail.
A blind commander turns the wheel,
and God on board becomes a fool,
screaming that we will fail,
that Tsushima will be our foil,
that madmen and baboons will fill
our fleet, and live to hear our knell,
that we will dine on our own bile
and sell our lives for coal.

# The Life and Death (and Life) of Galoom

Yellow. A swirl of asters. Cry "galoom"
so that the newborn spheres may have their laughs.
A strange beginning. Twist your brows. Could this
absence of sense mean swift imploding sense,
junipers, windy wilds, a swirling sphere,
Neptune ablaze? I think so. So I am.

No, it's not fair. You ask me who I am?
You see, I come from Neptune, where "galoom"
jumps from the cries of horses, whom the sphere
severed from their own speech. An island laughs:
an island of wild horses, robbed of sense,
a sense of islandness, wilder than this.

A loneliness. Aha! You figure this
notion will blaze the way to where I am?
A detour, nothing more. If you can sense
years of lost music in the word "galoom,"
soon you will hear the yellow in the laughs:
jaundiced flickers leaping from sphere to sphere.

Justice objects, saying: without a sphere,
a tale is nothing. I agree with this,
since comets, too, have tails. From ghoulish laughs
never will I spin yarns of who I am:
yearning to speak, I started with "galoom,"
and soon will sing the roundness and the sense.

As I remember how we swirled, I sense
just how your sounds have jostled with this sphere.
Yell out your rhythms. If the word "galoom,"
awkward at first, boldens, then think of this:
not from Neptune did I learn where I am.
Silence taught me, and swirls of foreign laughs.

So stumbling leads to sense. Loneliness laughs,
and slowly this strange room starts to make sense.
No harm in that. To find out who I am,
just ask me for a light. A glowing sphere,
astonished, reddens. Could it be that this
yawning planet has room for my galoom?

Vitally red. A sphere of asters tinged
with questions. Radiant iambic sense!
My poor galoom. A lightened language laughs.

## Looking Glass

How things can turn around.
It took only an unlikely
mirror, a face unlike
yours, gentler, more rotund,

but with that softening
effect a look of pain can have
when stony, turned inward: a cave
walled off. Often stinging

screams have drowned themselves here:
I love him! -- whispered like curled ferns
cut by my fingernails -- unfurled
kernels of tears. Other

grains, too, turn to green rain,
and the rain becomes beads for all
maples and sycamores laughing
to sweep up; the marred grass

will perk up. I give you
this gusty dawn, glow against glow
near the South Ferry, where billows
disturb still buildings, glue

loosened by fluid. Him
I'll leave sleeping; his scalp I'll not
stroke as you do. Old lies and plots
play awhile in the dim

bedroom, but the sun makes
mirrors of these. You can guess how
joyfully the light leaps in glass
won without burns or cuts,

stunning you with the sight
of others so unlike yourself,
form fighting through them, as all false
faces die into white.

# Notes for a Course in Phonology

Can I ignore the flagellant good-byes
of flailing trees, who lose as they embrace?
Can I forget the flicker on your face,
the green and blue and auburn in your eyes?
Or will I let it seize me by surprise,
that scoundrel death, who leaves without a trace,
snapping the golden thread that you have spun,
*that different reason in the rising sun?*

The dance begins with sounds.
Step back, and let the feet perform for you.
The vowels make their rounds.

Some come into the light,
knocking the rest into a different hue.
The pattern blurs my sight;

the artist, steeped in rage,
soaking the paintbrush, draws it lone and stark
across an empty page.

The student is a fool
who disregards the reasons in the dark
to memorize the rule.

The consonants in pairs
come forth, some gliding stoplessly,
the others taking chairs.

Some hold the hands of ghosts,
whose flesh and form can come to be
a question of the company
invited by the hosts.

I envy linguists, chemists, the wealthy ones,
the immortal ones. Peering into the gesture,
breaking the leaves into their particles,
they see the seasons as contiguous,
and similar, and not so harsh. I can't--
I myself crumble,
for I see the grace
of your veins, your lonely singleness of shape,
your lonely colors. I will hold you close
and whole. The time for dust has not arrived,
though it is near. Then I will hold the dust.
*A different reason in the rising sun.*

*the reasons in the rising*
*the guises of the seasons*
*the rise and fall of tidings*
*the crumbling of our reasons*
*the reasons for the fall*
*the falling of the seas*
*the risings of the tide*
*the dying of the trees*
*the scarlet in your eyes*
*the scars the stains the sores*
*(would I give up your glance*
*to analyze your pores?)*

Two suns rise together, for different reasons,
and meet. One sees an endless beginning,
and therefore begins with the end: dust,
ghostly with life. Time never ends
in this golden light, nor does it ever begin.
The other sees an end barely beginning,
a trap of beginning and end, embracing you,
dear dying one, dear urgent living one.

My page is blank with forms, yours filled with formulae.
They fall like leaves from the sun,
missing each other's reasons.

# Reunion

Lipstick, rings, sweat, glitches, beer, trophies,
innumerable vines drooping from tall tales.
Protecting our attentions, cold we tally

a purplish gryphon clambering through the mass
of clinks and wows, happily decapitated.
Thumping and clawful-lonesome, it ruins the fish,

spills someone's joke, muddies up the medley,
hurling a bunch of thick guilts around,
like messy neutrons, balanced only barely.

I start noticing we're standing on sand,
all tiny reunions whining to go home.
You can't be too careful. Somewhere around

the inside of my left elbow a critter scampers.
We buzz around each other swatting flies,
you and I, going foreign on each other.

The appetizers start snoring on death row.
Meanwhile the arch-creature, reaching the middle,
stands stock still and bows a genteel bow.

No, wait, look, it's Annie. You remember her.
Care for something, Annie? She deflects the question,
lifts off, tilts, and flaps easily through us,

a heathen headed for the ineffable clover.
We look around, scratching, starting to notice
uncomfortable things about ourselves and others.

We don't mention any of these things.
We guard the jagged pebbles between our toes.
Someone's daughter is standing on her head,
and our patch of sky is decked with dangling troubles.

## Ride Home

I burrow into your story of the rain
tapping its words darker than heroin.
This is where it began: a mistake,
a dumb lake, a well-intended walk;
this is where it ended: a cloud,
flexing itself over the snail-curled dead.
Your simple eyes I look up to for help,
your yarned-up raven head-mop, for sleep;
pillow me deep, dishevel me hard down
into the blood-bird's throat, leave me alone.

Tie my soul to a stone, explain a song,
tilting it on your cracked and chuckling tongue,
lead me to the playroom with the creaking chest,
yank out the blockhead toys, rehearse the cast,
daze me out riding on your ghost-spun wheels,
dizzy me snorkeling down through the colored coils
of your twizzled mind, where cops and spies grow wild,
and road trips tremble weird and cold.
Grinning to your sparse speech let me stretch mad,
slightly afraid, this far-fetched phony ride.

# Tower Song

Easy it seems
Not so. Once
over the under
I saw that neither the soil
longed for me, nor the air.
Go strum yourself asunder,
I said, then stretch
taut each single string
so that chords may be raised, hard
and faceted. Tall, glistening in sunset copper.
Cast away the wobbly shapes,
the flimsy matter. No longer
revel in a single face;
even the best of plans
become lines when tilted in a certain way,
or a line, when tilted, becomes a glance,
resonant, as glances tend to be,
hopeless, as no line can have a hope,
pointless, stretching beyond all other lines,
even beyond music, even beyond
sunsets and thunder, or frenzied clouds of murky birds,
or all the rubble you brought hailing down around,
just by asking me things, telling me things about towers.

## Upon Returning from a Leave of Absence

Though each word breaks into
panic, and touching hands recoil
like springs, and none of us can claim
a thing, and the dear name,

falling from our lips, meets the soil,
this has nothing to do
with hunger. Watch the rain:
it seeps through flimsy fingers, yet

stays where the earth has its fist
clenched. Wherever rain is missed,
fists are tougher. Nature in debt
makes one wealthy. Explain

why the homeless old man,
finding a shanty, heats it more
than we our fireplaces, why
the cactus holds water. Try

to build, to hold something that you're
used to wasting. You can,
if you give up all hope,
head brutally for the dry air,

learn how to cup your hands tight,
learn how to listen for light,
and return to view your despair
under a microscope.

# Acknowledgements, Credits, and Notes

I am grateful to Serving House Books and particularly to William K. Lawrence, its publisher, for encouraging, supporting, and publishing this book. Many thanks to all those who read and commented on the manuscript.

"A Concert at the Reformed Music Festival on Bakáts Square, Budapest" was first published in *Lowestoft Chronicle* (December 1, 2024). "Gyere, gyere közelebb" means "Come, come closer."

"Letters from a Doll" was published in *Broken Tribe Review*, (2024).

"The Bargain" was first published in *Eunoia Review*, May 20, 2024.

"Afternoon Visit" first appeared in 2014 in *Kol Hadash*, a publication of Congregation B'nai Jeshurun in New York City. "Odeh la-El levav hoker" means approximately, "I thank the God that probes all hearts."

"The Speech" was first published in my book *Republic of Noise: The Loss of Solitude in Schools and Culture* (R&L Education, 2012).

"Ride Home" appeared in *Sí Señor*, volume 1 (2002). (I founded *Sí Señor* and ran it for five years.) Before that, it was published on a poetry website that has since vanished, whose name I no longer recall.

The following poems were first published in the *Yale Literary Magazine*: "Coffee Psalm" (Fall 1990), "Notes for a Course in Phonology" (Spring 1991).

The following poems were first published in *Zirkus* (a Yale literary magazine): "Embarking from Libau" (Fall 1989), "Tower Song" (Winter 1992), "The Life and Death (and Life) of Galoom" (Spring 1992).

A number of the poems have appeared on my blog but are no longer visible there.

"Echoes of Sparrows" alludes to "Still, Citizen Sparrow" by Richard Wilbur.

The phrase "holy gadflies" in "Day of Rage" was suggested by Jon Awbrey.

## ABOUT THE AUTHOR

**Diana Senechal** is the 2011 winner of the Hiett Prize in the Humanities and the author of two books of nonfiction, *Republic of Noise* (2012) and *Mind over Memes* (2018), as well as numerous poems, stories, essays, songs, and translations. Her translations of the poetry of Tomas Venclova have been featured in two books *Winter Dialogue*, (1997) and *The Junction*, 2008); her translation of Gyula Jenei's poetry collection *Mindig más* (*Always Different: Poems of Memory*) was published in 2022 by Deep Vellum. She is currently working on a book about the songwriting partnership of Tamás Cseh and Géza Bereményi. Since 2017 she has been teaching at the Varga Katalin Gimnázium in Szolnok; in 2024 she served as the president of the Association of Literary Scholars, Critics, and Writers. For more about her work, see her website dianasenechal.com.

www.ingramcontent.com/pod-product-compliance
Lightning Source LLC
Chambersburg PA
CBHW060538080526
44586CB00012B/780